# GOOD NEWS

## HOPE AND ENCOURAGEMENT FOR TRYING TIMES

JUSTIN BARCLAY

# CONTENTS

*To my world, Lizzie and Ada Grace.*
*God has blessed me with such sweet reminders of His love.*

# INTRODUCTION

"Something's wrong."

Lizzie woke me out of deep sleep at three o'clock in the morning. I'll never forget those words. They set off a chain of events that would not let up for another 77 days.

She was 27 weeks pregnant, and we were expecting our first. It had been a relatively uneventful pregnancy up until then unless you count the craziness that enveloped the entire year. The world shut down. The chaos of a summer filled with riots in the streets. 2020 won't be soon forgotten.

Being pregnant during a global pandemic is challenging enough. But what we were about to discover is that things were only going to get more interesting.

Her water broke.

Early.

In fact, it was three months early.

We were excited to meet our little girl, but this was far too soon.

We called the doctor's 24-hour hotline when a nurse answered. Lizzie described what she was experiencing, and that's when we heard it. "Come to the hospital and pack a bag. You're going to be there for a while."

Even in that frantic moment, I remember a sense of calm.

Peace.

We got our things together and drove off into the night.

We were ushered into triage when we got to the hospital—greeted by a lovely nurse and a doctor who examined Lizzie. They asked plenty of questions and performed several procedures to monitor mother and baby. Eventually, they prepared us for the possibility that our little one was coming much sooner than expected. She might even be born that day. A specialist even came in at one point to prepare us for the list of possibilities. Worst-case scenarios. None that anyone would ever want to entertain when your baby is born at 27 weeks.

As I look back, the entire year seems like it was one thing after another. Many of us felt the same. We moved from one crisis to another. There was barely enough time to even come up for air.

At times I felt it too. But there was something different.

We felt the ups and downs, but there was a solid thread holding it all together.

Good news.

I've witnessed the same throughout my entire life as I look back on the pieces. The major moments and the minor memories, the dots always connect.

Steve Jobs, in his famous commencement speech at Stanford University, warned graduates about this strange phenomenon.

*"You can't connect the dots looking forward; you can only connect them looking backward. So you have to trust that the dots will somehow connect in your future. You have to trust in something — your gut, destiny, life, karma, whatever. Believing that the dots will connect down the road will give you the confidence to follow your heart even when it leads you off the well-worn path, and that will make all the difference." – Steve Jobs*

Throughout my life, I've seen the dots connect. A purpose for the pain. A reason for every season. Through deep reflection, I've come to realize that God has always been there.

And this year was no exception. We could feel His hand.

And that's good news.

The kind we don't often hear on the local nightly news. We very rarely see it printed in the paper. It's shared even less frequently by the big corporate media outfits in blogs or social media.

Have you ever wondered why?

The answer is simple and maybe not be as sinister as one might think. But why would the talking heads and reporters want to hide the good?

In some cases, they may flat out ignore what they disagree with. In others, they just aren't incentivized to seek it out. In all reality, they don't believe it sells. They subscribe to the theory that produces a constant daily drip of negativity into your feed. If it's a threat, they can sell it. It's their business model. If you depend on them to keep you safe, you'll stick around longer and keep coming back for more. Thus, they can sell more commercials and charge more for each one. In essence, they want your attention. And they've resorted to specific tactics to attract and retain it. Why do they do it? Because it works. But it doesn't have to be that way. You can break the news cycle. I'll show you how.

First, you must know that there is good news that you're just not being told about. Once you are aware of this simple fact, you'll spot it every day. See it everywhere you look. Soon, you'll be on the lookout for it.

There are simple strategies that work every time. I've been using them for years as someone who's had to constantly stay up to date on what's happening in the world. I've had to learn. I must look at more news every day than most folks read all year. That can be a depressing job if you're not intentional. It can beat you down and leave you feeling cynical. If you're not careful, you'll be feeling hopeless in a lost world.

I've found myself there once or twice. It's not fun. But it's avoidable. And I'd argue that it's more important to learn how to master this skill than ever before. To be clear, I'm not saying you should stick your head in the sand like an ostrich and pretend everything is all sunshine and rainbows.

On the contrary, it's wise to be informed. But even more critical, empowered. That's the goal of this book. What I'm talking about here is sifting through the noise to find news you can use. Never let it use you.

Each day I put these practical steps to work. And they do. I'm happy and healthy. Through the chaos of the last year, I've found a way to thrive through it all. Not just survive. We've been blessed beyond imagination. And I know you will be too. Because these strange but straightforward strategies are easy to use, you can put them to work immediately to start shifting the way you see the world and taking control of it today.

What if I told you that no matter what was happening in the world or your life, that it's possible to have peace through it all?

I've felt it. In the hospital. When the doctors sat us down and gave us the talk, back in 2012 when I was fired from what I thought was my dream job. Multiple times throughout my life, what was happening looked like complete and utter loss and failure. I learned not to trust specific reports, and instead, I put my faith in a higher power.

If any of this sounds too good to be true, just hear me out. I may not have believed it at one point in my life either. But I do now because I've lived it. I've seen the fruit.

If you'd like to have that peace in your life, too, then keep reading. If not, that's ok too. If you're fine where you are, then put this book down right now. Don't waste another minute. But on the other hand, if you're curious. If you've been praying for a better way, let's discover it together.

You've already made it farther than most. Many folks don't even crack open a book after they buy it.

According to the Pew Research group, roughly a quarter of Americans don't even read books at all. In 2018, they showed that 24 percent of American adults haven't read anything in the past year. Not an actual physical, ebook, or audio. On top of that, they found a dramatic correlation between wealth and education. The more you read, the more likely you are to earn more.

Yes, it pays to keep reading! And while you're here, that includes this book.

But far beyond financial gain, I know that you'll

gain something of even greater value if you do. Something priceless.

I get that I'm making some pretty significant claims. And I'm willing to back them up. But be warned, If you put this book down now, nothing changes. If you don't read and discover these simple solutions and, most importantly, put them into practice, you're doomed to stay enslaved.

On the following pages, I'll begin to break it all down in greater detail. I'll give you the good news and the bad. I won't pull any punches. I'll tell you the truth. And that's rare these days.

But most importantly, I'll give you the practical steps to take greater control of your life in the areas that matter most. So, now that we've gotten that out of the way. Where should we start?

What do you want to hear first?

1
___

## GOOD NEWS / BAD NEWS

"I've got good news and bad news. Which one do you want to hear first?"

The bad news is, it's bad. We live in a fallen world. Evil exists. Often it seems like it may be winning. The world can seem like a dark place. That's because it usually is. Ever since Eve took a bite of that forbidden fruit and passed it to Adam, it would be naive and reckless, quite frankly, to ignore it.

Bad things happen, and bad people are committing evil acts daily.

> "For we wrestle not against flesh and
> blood, but against principalities,
> against powers, against the rulers
> of the darkness of this world,

against spiritual wickedness in
high places." - Ephesians
6:12 KJV

Although, we live in a fallen world, and chaos
constantly swirls around us. There is hope. Because
even in the midst of the storm, God is making a way
through it all. He doesn't cause chaos, but he makes a
way through in spite of it.

## ALL THINGS

"And we know that in all things God
works for the good of those who
love him, who have been called
according to his purpose." -
Romans 8:28 NIV

The beauty of this verse is that it promises a
couple of things. First, no matter what happens, God
can shift it for good. You can have hope in the
promise that even though evil is present in the world
and bad things will happen to you, God can and will
use them for good in your life and the world. That's
powerful.

Nothing will prepare you to spend 77 days in the
NICU with your newborn baby seeing her strapped
down with cords and wires and tubes running into

her mouth. When Lizzie's water broke, we didn't know what to expect. It certainly wasn't our plan to spend that time over Christmas in the hospital. We were looking forward to spending  a festive holiday together with family, celebrating the pregnancy of our firstborn, and basking in the glow.

But God had a different plan. Ada Grace came early. And thank God because later, when we met with Lizzie's doctor, she told us some things about the birth that we didn't know. There were some complications that we just weren't aware of. Because of these specific issues, the OB said she wasn't sure what would've happened if our little girl had been carried to term. The word she used was pretty specific. She said it was a 'miracle.'

Now, I don't know if you know much about doctors. But that's not a word they like to throw around much.

She confirmed what we already knew. At 2 pounds 6 ounces, little Miss Ada Grace was and is a living, breathing miracle. What made it possible was God's grace. The skilled hands of the doctors and nurses and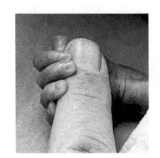

one of the best children's hospitals in the country that just so happened to be right in our back yard.

We often would meet parents during our stay and hear of others who made trips that took several hours back and forth to visit their children. They came from all over the state. Our trips only took 15 minutes. We were constantly confronted and convicted with stories that made us realize the blessings we were experiencing at every turn.

Ada's hospital room was large. It was much larger than a standard room. It was lined on two sides with eight baby incubators. Super high-tech beds that controlled temperature and even humidity for the babies. When they're born that early their skin isn't entirely done forming. They require a more humid atmosphere to keep their sensitive skin 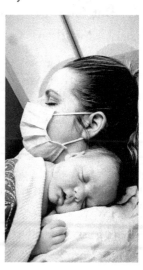 from tearing while it continues to come together. It was a powerful gift to be able to watch our little one being knit together by God. Piece by piece, she was being shaped by His hands, right in front of our very eyes. We would never have chosen this path, but we were grateful for those steps along the way.

There was a little girl who was across from us in that room. She was born with a rare condition. Her intestines were outside of her body. As scary as that sounds, the doctors had seen it before. They could calmly assess her situation and bring her and her parents peace as they worked to make her comfortable. They performed a special surgery to put her intestines into her body where they belonged and sewed her up.

As you could imagine, she was in quite a bit of pain for a while and needed medication. Her parents weren't able to hold her for some time. Though eventually, they would be able to not only hold her but take her home.

We were constantly showered and sometimes pelted with little reminders of God's presence and promises through it all.

I can't begin to know what the family of that little girl was going through. I can tell you what we faced, and while I wouldn't wish it on anyone, I'm grateful that we weren't alone.

We were surrounded by caring and experienced professionals who walked alongside us—many other parents in the same boat. But most of all, a loving God who never left us.

If God can work good in all things, what was he working in the midst of this? What did he do with our little one? What about the sweet girl who was born with that unusual condition and her parents? Or parents who've lost a child?

I can't pretend to have all of the answers. That's way above my pay grade. I just don't. But there's one thing I do know. In times of great tragedy and sorrow and seasons of celebration, you are not alone. We are never alone through the good and the bad. A higher power is working behind the scenes.

In our case, I can tell you that we learned some powerful lessons right upfront. As Lizzie and I looked at each other during this challenging time, we both realized that if we could make it through this, we could make it through almost anything. We had never been closer to one another. And we had never been closer to God. It's a different sort of prayer that a parent prays when a child's life is on the line.

Yes, we live in a fallen world. But we believe in a risen Christ. One who paid the price for our salvation. That means he transcended all of the chaos, pain, and brokenness of the world. And we can too. Through Him, we have hope and love. There is light in the darkness and calm in the chaos. No matter what our circumstances, in the world, we know that God is good. And He's constantly working good in and through all things.

It's one thing for me to say, but it's a whole other issue for you to see it. How do you discover the good in such an evil world?

Can you create it?

What would it look like?

In the coming pages, I'll show you how I've been able to do just that, and I believe you can too. But first, I want to tell you a little bit more about what we're up against and, more importantly, who's on our side.

It's a good idea to know what we're facing, but it's even more important to know, the battle is already won.

## 2

## BAD NEWS TRAVELS FAST

Cruising down the freeway, Al and his friend were out for a ride. Even though it was a summer evening in LA, they seemingly had the whole road to themselves. That is until, of course, Al happened to look back in his rearview mirror. There he saw a sight that would be hard to imagine. At a glance, he saw the flashing lights of more than a dozen police cars, and with another, he saw his best friend holding a gun. This was no leisurely afternoon drive. This ride would change the course of TV news in America and drive ratings through the roof for a certain network. Al Cowlings and Oj Simpson coated along in the infamous white Bronco as the news sped across the world.

Remember the old saying; bad news travels fast? Well, these days, it travels at the speed of light and sometimes even quicker. The rise of the internet and social media allows everything to go viral with just a few clicks.

As much good as the internet and social media have brought us, they both come with their fair share of troubles too. We take the good with the bad. It's just like when man discovered fire. I bet that first interaction was a doozy. Electricity was the same way. Edison revealed that electricity was so powerful that it could cook the food or the man. The power lies not in technology but in the way we use it.

This technology could easily be used to spread good news throughout the world. And make no mistake, it is. But it can also be used to divide and destroy.

That's a very sobering reality, especially when it comes to news; or the flow of information.

It used to be that you had time to chew on the news of the day. It wasn't long ago when you read the newspaper with your morning coffee. Some places got a morning and an afternoon paper. That's a lot of news! But not compared to what we're bombarded with today. Back in those days, we could chew on what we were reading. Give it time to digest. We didn't feel the need to instantly form an opinion and immediately line up with a particular camp. We had time to respond vs. react.

Radio and television soon emerged, and along with it, the 24-hour cable news network. Unlike the newspapers who only had room to print certain things, the networks had more time than ever. And it had to be filled. What happens when you have a slow news day? Do they turn off the feed and go home? Not at all. This new space for content demanded to be filled. They had to feed the beast! And this beast has an insatiable appetite. News producers went searching for more. And sure enough, they found it. Sometimes it found them.

Just like that summer night back in 1994 with OJ and Al in the white Bronco. We were all watching the slow-speed chase on that highway in Southern California because news networks had something to run with. And it was gold. Many local tv stations in LA still run car chases to this day because they're rating bonanzas.

Soon more and more cable networks would pop up, and eventually, blogs came along. And what went from a 24-hour news cycle eventually became instant insanity virtually overnight. Reporters only had the space of a newspaper to fill at one point and a half an hour newscast on local or national tv. Then, 24-hour networks. Now, they faced a new and exciting challenge; endless room for news.

Blogs have no limit to what can be written. Their only challenge is how fast they can get the information out. It's a race to first, not facts. And because of the constant flow of headlines, it's often buried when the truth comes out because these so-called news organizations have moved on to the next serving of the day—the outrageous meme of the moment.

These things dramatically changed our diet when it comes to news. Before we were served up limited offerings like meals, soon, we'd have an endless buffet to gorge on. That's where we find ourselves today. Bloated. We're stuffed with information. Most of it is lacking any real relevance or nutritional value. All of it specifically crafted to evoke a reaction and reinforce a narrative. Each produced for a targeted audience.

What it often boils down to is pure distraction. It divides us, and we are conquered. We have very little chance to unite, even among issues that we would likely find ourselves agreeing on.

We're lead astray by those whose business model counts on our outrage. It plays on our division. It keeps us battling each other when the real enemy is free to play.

With all of these changes happening in the blink of an eye, how do you fight back?

The first step is awareness. You must know what the truth is. The reality is that these sources aren't always interested in getting it right. For the most part, they're not serving you. They have separate interests. Knowing how the sausage is made gives you the tools to be empowered, not just informed. That's a powerful thing. Eventually, you'll begin to see through the fog to what's going on.

If you're reading this book, chances are you already have. Listeners to my daily radio show and podcast know what I mean. Each day I try to cut through the noise and give people the real news. It's my goal to bring them stories that they may not hear anywhere else. I share Accounts that are being ignored and entirely left out of the official feed.

They say, 'if it bleeds, it leads," which means news organizations always lead with the bad news first. They believe it hooks you in. Some of that may be true. It sure seemed to be the case with that slow-speed chase with OJ and Al. It may be the way we're wired. We assess threats around us. It's a unique design that keeps us on our toes. And while bad news travels fast these days, it's essential to follow up with the good. It's the duty and responsibility of everyone reporting, whether on radio, tv, or the internet, to give you a complete picture of what's going on, ideally, without bias.

A complete picture comes with the good, the bad, and the ugly. Often we hear the bad and the ugly, but the good is nowhere to be found. That's just irresponsible.

So, how does it all work? I'll give you a bit of an inside look. I believe the more you know, the better prepared you'll be to spot it when you see it.

Let's start with something that isn't news, to begin with, the weather.

## 3

## THE FORECAST

*"It's right on top of us! Everyone take cover."*

I 've worked in radio since I was in high school. My first night on the job was Christmas Eve. They still needed an actual person to play music and keep the radio station on the air back then. Nowadays, they have computers for that. At nearly all of the radio stations across the country, there's nobody there overnight. But back in 1996, I was.

And I was at work that day too, January 3, 2000. It was right in the middle of the afternoon drive. It was the time when people would usually be driving home or picking up the kids at school. But today, a tornado warning had just been issued, and the town of Owensboro, KY, where the radio station I worked for was located, was bracing for a big one.

Jimmy was tracking it on the radar. We could see

it moving block by block. Back then, we had a computer screen inside the studio with radar specifically used for the radio station. It was pretty similar to what you might see when you pull up an app on your smartphone today. But this system was more powerful.

We could see the tornado cutting a path through town. Jimmy was giving the directions, and updates to people live on the air. I still remember him calling out neighborhoods and tracking the twister street by street. Until, finally, it was there, right on top of us.

When we got the call to take cover, we all moved to a room in the center without windows, ducking under the desk. Before we did, I got a chance to take a glance out the back door, and what I saw, I'll never forget. The cars in the parking lot were bouncing up and down. It was dark. And you could feel a pressure in the air like I'd never felt before.

It all happened very quickly but seemed to move slowly as well. It's hard to explain, but time tends to slow down in situations like that. It almost drags along.

I remember when we all crawled out from underneath the desk and emerged from that little room. We started getting reports of the aftermath phoned in. Thankfully, our building had been spared. But just across the street, the old college had taken a direct hit. Huge hundred-year-old trees were ripped up by their roots. Old stately brick buildings were demolished.

As I made my way out of town and back home that night, I got a first-hand tour of the devastation. A roof ripped off of a school gymnasium. Half of a grocery store just vanished. And in one neighborhood, so much destruction that one first responder guessed maybe 100 lives had been lost.

But that thankfully just wasn't true.

Even though the F3 tornado ripped through town, destroying over 100 homes and causing more than $70 Million in damage, thankfully, there were no fatalities. Only 18 were injured during the prime rush-hour time. It was truly a miracle.

But I also believe God had a little help that day. My good friend Jimmy and the rest of the broadcast professionals tracked the storm and reported accurate information moment by moment to keep the citizens informed. Oh, I'm sure the ratings were sky-high that day, but that didn't seem to matter much. What these folks were focused on was saving lives. And I believe they did.

That's a stark contrast to the hype we experience these days.

Recently, even the Weather Channel has gotten in on the act.

*"Ever since the 2012-2013 winter season, The Weather Channel (TWC) has given every*

*significant winter storm event it forecasts and tracks a unique name. Their argument for doing this? "It's simply easier to communicate about a complex storm if it has a name," says TWC hurricane specialist Bryan Norcross. Even so, an official system for naming winter storms has never existed in the United States."[1]*

But could there possibly be something more to this phenomenon? What about the fear factor?

Keeping the public informed is one thing, but it's another to keep them in a constant state of fear and dependent on your product for relief. That's bondage.

The Weather Channel folks are guilty. They've been hyping up weather events to keep us tuned in. See, the longer we watch, the more money they make. Their ratings go up, and they can charge advertisers more. The people who fund these operations have soap to sell. And baby food, dog food, and deodorant. You name it. Their marketing messages tend to hit harder when the audience is already susceptible and cowering in fear.

When we're in a constant state of fear, we don't make rational decisions. We are easily manipulated and controlled. We buy more soap, dog food, and deodorant. But we also buy into promises from politicians to make it all better. Despite their poor track record, we give up our power without a fight in exchange for the trade-off that they will solve all of our problems. How long have they been fighting the war on poverty or the war on drugs? A simple vote for the politician who promises to make your pain go away is made possible from carefully calculated messages crafted by high-powered marketing and PR firms. This can be a real danger when we don't realize what the consequences are.

Fear can be contagious and corrosive. But not all fear is bad. There is a difference between danger and fear. It can be a productive and healthy signal that danger lies ahead. Danger should be respected. That's prudent and wise. But when fear is abused, it can be an unhealthy addiction.

Fear is a liar. It's often a form of worship. Simply put, it's faith in the wrong thing.

Let me say that again. Fear is faith in the wrong thing.

The constant imagining of the worst-case scenario gives us a false illusion that somehow we're in control. It makes us feel like because we've examined all of the possibilities, we're somehow better prepared for what may come our way. And that's just not true. Because most of the time, the kind of fear I'm talking about produces no real action or adequate response. In reality, it creates the opposite—a society crippled by anxiety. We're left paralyzed in the wake of messages that leave us feeling hopeless, helpless, and lost.

So, what can you do? Should you turn your tv off altogether? Is it time to chuck your smartphone and never tune in again? How do you find the balance?

That would be unreasonable and indeed not wise. I'm not suggesting sticking your head in the sand like an ostrich. It's essential to be informed. That can be empowering if you have all of the facts. Just remember that you're often not getting the whole picture. Whoever is writing, announcing, or producing the news you're consuming has a plan.

It's essential to be plugged in because the information has the power to be empowering. In fact, like that day, the tornado swept through town, I believe it can save lives. It did that day. But something happens when this trust is abused. Just like the story of chicken little, who claimed the sky was falling, eventually, folks stop listening.

A fresh new report was just released at the time I'm writing this.

*"The U.S. ranks last among 46 countries in trust in media, Reuters Institute report finds"*

Just 29% of people surveyed in the U.S. said they trust the news. That's worse than Poland, the Philippines, and Peru. The report comes from the Reuters Institute for the Study of Journalism at Oxford. Where the study also found some improvement in trust in nearly all countries. It's believed that's because of COVID-19 coverage. But not in the U.S. Out of all the local topics covered, the weather had the highest interest level.

It's most likely because it has the most immediate and direct impact on us each day. Will it rain? Do I need to bring an umbrella to work? What about that snowstorm? We've come to depend on this information, and we hold the folks who report it to a higher standard. That's because we can confirm it right away.

We have no idea when the other reporters are lying to us or just plain leaving things out.

It's kind of hard to fake the weather. But rain, snow, sleet, or hail; no matter what the weatherman says, you can always find peace in the storm.

---

1. *https://www.thoughtco.com/why-the-weather-channel-names-winter-storms-3444521*

## 4

## THE CALM IN THE STORM

T wo thousand years ago, a few men were riding in a boat when a storm came upon them seemingly out of nowhere. It tossed the rickety little craft back and forth on the waves. These men were obviously shaken up. They were out alone in the water in a tiny boat that they were afraid just wouldn't hold up or, worse, might capsize, and they'd all be thrown overboard into the churning and angry sea.

But they forgot one tiny but essential detail. They weren't alone. Even though the forecast looked grim. The storm was raging out of control. These men completely ignored the fact that they had a weapon in the war with their circumstances. Jesus.

These men were Disciples, and they had just left a crowd of people where Jesus was performing miracles. He was healing the sick and even casting out demons. They had seen it all. So, why in the middle of their own storm did they completely forget about the one who was with them who had the power to change it all?

He was sleeping. When the Disciples woke him up, they plead with him, "Lord save us! We're going down!"

The Bible simply says Jesus got up and *"rebuked the winds and waves, and it was completely calm."*

But before He did, he looked at the men and said, *"You of little faith, why are you so afraid?"*

How often in our own lives do we encounter storms of our own only to forget the promises made entirely. How often do we lose sight of the fact that no matter how hard the wind whips and the rain rages, that we are not alone.

If these men who walked and talked with Jesus and had just seen him moments before performing miracle after miracle could lose sight of his awesome power, we can too. I guess we shouldn't be too hard on ourselves.

Don't completely ignore the forecast. That would be foolish. We must know that storms are coming our way, just like they always have. As I laid out earlier, we live in a fallen world. But we have a super-power—the Truth and redemption.

It's a great reminder not to focus on the forecast. It's good to know what's predicted, but it's even better to know what's promised. That's wisdom.

When Lizzie and I spent those 77 days in the hospital driving back and forth, one thing that kept us going was faith. Like a magnet, it pulled us through the storm. We did our best not to focus on how dire our circumstances might have been during that time. To the outside world or the untrained eye of little faith, they were less than ideal. Let's be honest; they were downright scary. We had some real shaky moments at times. But we focused on faith.

One of the best things you can do with your baby in the NICU is simply holding her. They call it 'Kangaroo care' or skin to skin. We each took turns to strip off our shirts. We'd lay little 2-pound six-ounce Ada Grace on our chest and cover up with a blanket. It felt every bit as amazing as you could imagine. In those moments, all was right with the world.

While we lay there together, my mind drifted off to a better time and place. I thanked God for the days to come when she would be wrapped up in my arms as we rocked in the hammock under the shade trees at our happy place, a little cottage on a small lake in Michigan. I could feel the breeze. I heard the birds chirping as I pictured the smile on my sweet baby's face. I focused on faith. The promise of peace. The calm in the storm.

As I write this today, little Miss Ada Grace just had her six-month check-up with the doctor. That tiny little bundle of joy is growing bigger and stronger every day. She's nearly fifteen pounds! Her doctor is so impressed with her growth and outcome that he often remarks how unusual it is. Maybe in the natural. But with my eyes fixed on how good God is, I can see clearly how blessed she is, and it's no surprise because I'm focused on faith. My eyes are on Jesus.

Spending all of that time in the hospital gave me a new perspective. It shifted my view.

Maybe peace isn't the world around you in a constant state of calm, but rather the feeling you experience *within* from the knowledge that *God is in control and still on the throne.*

### Jesus Calms The Storm

> *Then he got into the boat, and his disciples followed him. Suddenly a furious storm came up on the lake so that the waves swept over the ship. But Jesus was sleeping. The disciples went and woke him, saying, "Lord, save us! We're going to drown!"*
> *He replied, "You of little faith, why are you so afraid?" Then he got up and rebuked the winds and the waves, and it was completely calm. The men were amazed and*

asked, "What kind of man is this? Even the winds and the waves obey him!"

—-MATTHEW 8:23-27

## 5

## THE REST OF THE STORY

I t was a cold December day when Harry and his friend and coworker set off into the Oklahoma woods for a Sunday full of rabbit hunting. Little did they know, as they wrapped up the day's events, they would become the hunted.

As they returned to their car, the two were approached by three armed men in a Buick. They were about to be robbed at gunpoint. Acting quickly, Harry's friend, an off-duty Tulsa detective, raised his shotgun. He pulled the trigger. But the weapon misfired.

That's when the three would-be robbers started shooting.

Guns a-blazing.

Harry was hit. And so too was his friend.

Despite wounds in one lung, leg, and liver, he found the strength to drive to a nearby farmhouse, where he collapsed. Officer Harry Aurandt died from his injuries two days later. The Detective was left paralyzed for life.

Officer Harry Aurandt was survived by his wife, daughter, and two-year-old son.

His son would grow up without a father. Raised by his single mother, the boy would eventually serve in the Army Air Corps during WWII. He had a distinguished career. His service lasted 14 months.

But you may know him best for a profession that lasted far longer. One that got its start while he was in high school.

A teacher recognized the young man's voice. She was highly impressed with his pipes. Mrs. Isabelle Ronan was so moved that she took him to a local radio station to see about getting the 14-year-old a job.

The station manager must've taken a liking to the lad because he decided to let him in to help keep the place clean and perform odd jobs around the office. Eventually, they even allowed him to read commercials and, before long, the news.

And that's what the young man would become famous for.

Millions would tune in every day to hear his constant calm in the daily storm-a clear voice of reason. He delivered news and information that inspired and empowered millions while lifting a nation.

Paul Aurandt was a national treasure. He remains one of the most popular and beloved radio broadcasters of all time. But you may know him by his middle name, Harvey.

"Paul Harvey... Good day." The famous sign-off was heard by enormous audiences daily.

The impact Paul had on the lives of countless Americans is absolutely crystal clear. Just like his voice.

But even though his story didn't exactly have a happy beginning. It didn't end there.

I can't even imagine the challenges that he must've faced. His mother certainly had her work cut out for her.

And what was a rocky start could have lead to an even rougher road—a life of tragedy. But Paul Harvey's story didn't end there.

And no matter where you are now, you're still writing your very own. You have one heck of a co-author.

She stopped breathing. She was starting to turn a grayish-blue. I'm here to tell you that not much in life will prepare you for the moment your baby goes limp in your arms. Her heart stopped beating, and all of the life just seemed to drain from her body.

The nurses saw the notifications on the monitor and quickly sprang into action. I saw her hands shaking. She moved fast. I know they've seen it all in the NICU, but even the most skilled and seasoned veterans must experience a wave of panic when a baby is lying lifeless in her father's arms.

I can't logically tell you how and there is no reason on Earth to describe why, but I remained calm. It wasn't a shock. It wasn't trauma. But I felt a peace that just surpassed it all. Something larger and more significant than anything I've ever experienced. It's almost as if someone had His hand on my shoulder, looking down at us as I witnessed it all.

I watched as the nurses grabbed the oxygen mask and started to blow the cool air into our sweet little girl's face. This is called a blow-by in the NICU. The tube is hooked into the wall. It supplies clean oxygen directly to the patient. Usually, after a few seconds of air, they wake right up. Back to life from a moment of sleep. Sometimes the babies have to be patted sternly on the back. It jolts them back into reality.

That's when I heard it. The beeping tones of the monitor signaled her heart and breathing came back online. Our little girl was back. I won't speak for Lizzie, but I never had a doubt. It's what can only be described as "knowing."

Everything is going to be alright.

That is a feeling like no other on Earth. That's because it comes from an entirely different place.

No matter how bad it may seem. No matter what the monitors may signal.

When you think the verdict is in, and you know how it all ends. Just remember that there's more to your story. We're writing it as we go. No failure is final. Each tragedy may be only temporary. Although we face setbacks and profound challenges, we're not alone.

The same steps we take on our journey may lead to a path of purpose that only God can see in its full glory.

We won't have all the answers at the moment. We can't even pretend to. But we don't need them, after all. Not as long as we trust God's plan and have faith that He's working good through it all.

When you think you've seen the end, just remember the rest of the story.

**Q: Looking back, is there a time when you saw an incredible turn of events?**

When did God move powerfully and decisively in your life?

*If He's done it before, He can do it again.*

## 6

# THE GOOD NEWS

W hat's the good news? It's the news you won't hear anywhere else. Very rarely will you see it covered by the big corporate media. You won't watch it nightly on the networks. And you certainly won't see much of it written in the papers.

Simply put, The Good news is the truth—the absence of lies.

No matter what's going on in the world, there is always good to be found. But the source of it all is often ignored. What is the root of all that is good? God.

> Jesus answered, "I am the way and the
> truth and the life. No one comes
> to the Father except through me.

*— -JOHN* 14:6

The Gospel is the good news. It's the best news. The very meaning of the word is "good news." The Gospel is the message concerning Christ, the kingdom of God, and salvation. This story of actual life events is told in the first four books of the New Testament. It tells of the life, death, and resurrection of Jesus. The reason I share it with you is because it's the very foundation of who I am. It's at the core of my being. It's the source of all of my peace.

My faith impacts every area of my life. I can't imagine going through the last year without it. One thing is clear. As time marches on, uncertainty and chaos seem to rule the day. If 2020 has taught us anything, it's that all that we hold dear is up for grabs. Every tradition and every institution sits on a precarious perch. The very fabric that ties society together is under attack. It's being torn apart and ripped to shreds. All of this can seem like a frightening experience. And without God, it certainly is.

But *with* Jesus comes the courage to face it all. With His strength and peace, we can learn not just to survive but also to thrive. I know because I've seen it up close and personal.

Last year was a test for us all. The challenges were real. Many faced hardships, lost loved ones or their livelihood, and experienced pain on levels they'd never faced before. But as the world was seemingly starting to crumble, I had a thought that I can only attribute to God. I began to believe that even though on the surface things looked grim, God could and would use it all to bring us out stronger and better on the other side. In other words, even in the chaos, He could find a way to bless us.

Now, I know how crazy that sounds on the surface. When you're thinking in terms of the world, it often is. But the world has nothing on Jesus. He died to break us free from those chains. His death gave us the ultimate freedom. That redeeming power of Christ can turn burdens into blessings. And last year, that's precisely what I witnessed.

We were blessed in so many ways. Although the birth of our baby girl was a challenge, God used it to lift us up. We bought the home we live in, which not only saved us money each month on our payment but ultimately grew our net worth because the values have risen dramatically in the last year. Financially, we never lacked and never wanted anything.

These are real-world results. But they don't stop there. Our little girl is healthy and strong. She's growing bigger every day. Her doctor often remarks that he would've never known that she was born three months premature without looking at her chart.

I tell you all of this to say that the news of the world may point to a certain outcome, but the Good news of Jesus points the other way. We need to spend less time focused on the world and more time in the Word.

Only then can we see the truth and know the way.

## 7

## SEE THE GOOD

Seek and You Will Find

I had to have it. I can remember the first time I laid eyes on it. It was a car like I'd never seen before. It looked like a spaceship. The Toyota Celica I bought brand-new back in 2000 was one of my favorite cars. One of the things I loved most about it was that it didn't look like any other car on the road. That is until I drove it off the lot.

The moment I did, I started to see them everywhere.

Has that ever happened to you? It's pretty standard. This phenomenon is due to a gift. Each of us has it.

*"Ask and it will be given to you; seek and you will find; knock and the door will be opened to you. 8*

*For everyone who asks receives; the one who seeks
finds; and to the one who knocks, the door will be
opened.*

— -MATTHEW 7:7-8

It's a Biblical concept. But scientists have discovered something extraordinary about how we were created.

It starts above your spinal cord. About two inches long and the width of a pencil. A system that allows you to recognize patterns, amongst other things. This powerful piece of your body connects the subconscious part of your brain with the conscious. It's called the **Reticular Activating System**. It's an impressive-sounding name for a tiny section of the brain. Small but mighty. The RAS aids in attention, goal achievement, and keeping you alive. All of your senses, except for your sense of smell, are connected directly into this bundle of neurons that's about the size of your pinky.

Many times its function is compared to a bouncer at a nightclub. It's a filter that makes sure your brain doesn't have to deal with more information than it can handle at any given time. Your RAS determines your perception. And as they say, perception is reality.

Just like with cars, our brain can and will seek out what it is set to find. If you've ever been on a long road trip, chances are you've played the kids game, I-spy. *"I spy with my little eye...."* Older kids turned this game into *"Punch bug."* When you're driving for a long distance, the first person to see a Volkswagen Beatle, nicknamed Bug, yells out *"Punch Bug!"* and punches someone in the arm. I remember years of fun playing this game as a kid with my little brother in the backseat of our Chrysler station wagon. My parents probably don't have the same fondness for those memories.

The same system that drives that game can also determine what we focus on each day. For the most part, we don't even realize it. Most of us go through life on cruise control. We've set the autopilot, or it's been set for us. But we had no idea.

The good news is that once you understand this powerful phenomenon, it can become a serious tool.

What if you could determine the kind of day you would have? Most people go through life thinking that life just happens to us. They believe it's a series of random events stacking up each day that ultimately we have no power or control over. But that doesn't have to be true. Armed with this information, it should never be true again.

## Create & Find More Good

What if you could not only find more good in the world and your life but create it too? Just like the cars on the road, chances are it's there, but you haven't activated your RAS to pick it out just yet. Every day, you may be missing some of the most beautiful moments and the constantly occurring miracles. But the good news is, it's a simple fix. If you want to find more good, you must first focus on the good, just like the car.

The best place to start is with the good that's already there.

> *"Enter his gates with thanksgiving and his courts with praise; give thanks to him and praise his name."*

> — PSALM 100:4

This little verse is the key to it all. It completely describes how to not only find more good in your life but create it too. And it starts with gratitude. It begins with thanksgiving. Thanking God for the blessings already in your life can completely shift your entire perspective in a heartbeat.

Often, we walk through life with our heads hanging down. We've allowed something or someone to shift our focus. The solution is to lift your gaze to the one who created it all and is responsible for each and every amazing gift you and I have ever received.

You may say, but Justin, you don't know my situation. You just don't understand. My life is in shambles. Apply this same statement to the news of the world these days, and it may sound similar. I'm here to tell you that no matter how grim the story may sound, no matter how lost it all may seem, that God is still in control, and He's still on the throne. And that's good news.

Here's a challenge. Stop reading this right now, and write down three things that you're grateful for. Take a moment and just jot down three simple things. You don't have to think too hard about this. You probably shouldn't. Just write down the first three things that come to mind.

I'll show you three of mine.

1. **Coffee**
2. **Smiles from my sweet little Ada Grace**
3. **Sunrise**

We can always give thanks for something. Do you have electricity in your home? How about running water? Is it clean and hot?

Each morning when we get up and go into the bathroom to flip on the light switch and turn the shower on, we experience true gifts and miracles right before our very eyes. We see them so often that we take them for granted.

But all across the globe, people make the trek to a

well to collect water and bring it back to their homes. Yes, in 2021, this is still a common practice in some places. Can you imagine having to do that each day? People live in huts and with dirt floors, and we get all discombobulated when it takes our smartphone a few extra moments to pull down the latest pictures our friends have posted of their lunch online from the cloud.

We've completely lost perspective. It's easy to do when you live as we do. We have been blessed beyond measure, and we've lost perspective for it all. But through this little exercise, we can quickly re-focus and bring our attention back to God's glorious gifts.

After you've got your big 3, now, include why you're grateful for these things. A short sentence or two is fine. But you can go into as much depth and detail as you'd like. Often, I find that when I do this right. I really *feel* with all my heart the genuine grati-tude I experience for some of the simplest things or the people in my life. When you truly open up your heart to this experience, you will feel that connection as you praise God and give Him all of the glory for these gifts.

1. **Coffee** - Thank you, Jesus, for the hot cup of coffee I'm sipping on right now as I write this. I love the way it tastes and the energy that it gives me. It warms me

up from the inside out. Sometimes there's nothing better.

2. **Smiles from my sweet little Ada Grace** - Thank you, Lord, for this little miracle. When I see her face light up, it warms my heart. I thought I knew what love was before, but I honestly had no idea until that little gift came into my life.

3. **Sunrise** - Thank you, Father, for the feeling of renewal, refreshment, and restoration that's packed into every sunrise. It gives me hope for each new day. I love to witness the sun coming up in the morning as it trumpets your glory. A reminder that in a dark world, the light of your love always shines bright.

When you master this little exercise, eventually, it begins to click. You realize that every good thing comes from God. Each sunrise, each smile, even coffee. Sometimes the simplest treats can be the most treasured. When you recognize this simple truth, you can learn to praise God for every amazing experience in your life. You will start to see the abundance of the blessings already here and the possibility of what's to come.

I do this each morning, and it truly grounds me. Before I do anything else, I give God the first part of my day, and I always find that He takes care of the rest.

One more simple question. What would make today a fantastic day? Just jot down three things that would make today the best.

Here's my example for today.

1. **Writing**
2. **A nap in the rain**
3. **Time with Ada and Lizzie together**

Are you starting to see how simple this can be?

I'll break these down for you. I'm writing this on the weekend. It's Saturday. And it's raining. All-day. We would typically have some other adventure planned today. But for the most part, we'll be lying around the house. And these three will help me enjoy the day in the way I'd like to.

1. **Writing** - The most important project I need to focus on and complete today. I'm on a deadline, and I want to get this book done and into your hands as soon as possible!

2. **A nap in the rain** - This is a simple guilty pleasure. Nothing profound here, but it would make a pretty significant

impact. I'll probably do this when I need to take a break from writing.

3. **Time with Ada and Lizzie together** - This one is self-explanatory. I like to spend as much time as possible with these two. And anyone can see why. They're my world.

These three can be more complex and specific to some powerful goals you have in your life, or they can simply be a little glimpse of glory you'd like to experience today. They'll look different every day. And that's ok because each of us is in a different season.

By focusing on the good that's already there and giving thanks for the blessings, you're able to shift your perspective and see not only what glorious gifts you've been blessed with but also the experience and life you can create along the way.

## WARNING

You may be tempted because this sounds so simple. It's almost too simple. You may be tempted not even to try this. You may think to yourself that it sounds too good to be true. You may even feel like that this is a bunch of hogwash! Maybe it is. I don't know how it all works. I can only tell you that it does. I've seen it make a dramatic and profound impact on my life. I know the power that it has to make a difference. And that's why I share it with you. I challenge you to try it. Commit to this little routine over the next seven days. Start your day with this practice and see where it takes you. If you don't feel even a tiny difference in the next week, you can stop. But chances are, once you get going, you'll see what I mean. Your world will be a different place. So, give it a go. And let me know how it works for you. I'm excited to hear your story.

Email me: Blessings@justinbarclay.com

Download a free copy of my Good News Journal template today:

JustinBarclay.com/goodnewsjournal

## Good plan

*Write the three things that your most thankful for right now!*

1. _____

2. _____

3. _____

## 8

## CHOOSE GOOD

While you look for the good, make intentional choices about what you consume.

Take note of what the information and media you consume do to you.

How do they make you feel?

When I was much younger, I could stay up late. Eat pizza and tacos and even drink alcohol with little to no effect on me the next day. But when you hit a certain age, things change.

I can't do any of that anymore without feeling the consequences.

If I want to feel my best, I have to give my full attention to what I put in my body.

The same is true for what I take into my mind.

What are you watching, reading, listening to?

Are you scrolling through social media aimlessly?

Do you find yourself comparing yourself to others?

*How do you feel?*

Are you on the couch binging on Netflix?

I used to do that too. But I don't watch much tv these days.

How do you feel when you watch the nightly news or your favorite news show on cable tv?

In the media business, there's a reason why they call radio and television *programming*.

Each time you sit down to watch the news, a show or listen to a podcast, YOU are being programmed. Remember that and make those decisions intentionally.

The old saying, "garbage in / garbage out," is true.

Just like what you put in your physical body, what you allow into your mind matters too.

You cant expect to eat a steady diet of fast food and booze and perform like a world-class athlete. The same can be said for your mind.

### Q: How do you want to feel?

Start with the end in mind.

If you want to feel energized and ready to conquer the world and become the person God created you to be, what would you have to do? Think about who that is and what that looks like. What would that person do every day? What would they eat?

Would they spend their nights mindlessly binging through seasons of a tv show, or would they read a book or watch something that inspires them?

## Digital detox

Clippity Clop Clippity Clop. The horse's hooves have a rhythm all their own. They sing to you a serene melody that puts you at ease.

A few years ago, Lizzie and I took a trip up north to one of our favorite spots. It's a tiny island in between the straits of Mackinac (pronounced Mack-in-aw) and the upper and Lower Peninsula of Michigan. Mackinac Island. It's a magical place where only horses and bicycles are allowed on the streets. There are no cars, trucks, or motorized vehicles of any kind, except for the ambulance, the fire department, and police. But you hardly ever see them.

While away, I un-plugged. I just put my phone down. I didn't check my email; I didn't read the news; I didn't even look at Facebook. Would you believe that when we got done with the trip and came back, the world was still spinning? That's right. I put everything down, and it was all there still waiting for me when I came back. A *digital detox* has become more common in recent years. More and more people all over are putting their phones, their tablets, and their computers down, at least for a while. Whether you decide to make it for a day, a weekend, or even longer, a digital detox can do a lot to give your mind rest and restore your soul.

I learned a lot on that island. I learned to rest. I learned to slow down. It's so important because when you do, you'll start to see the world around you and what's happening when you're present with the ones you love. And most importantly, the things that matter most demand and receive your full attention.

## Burn out

Oh, I've been burned out many times in my life. It can feel like you're losing interest in almost everything. Losing all hope and feeling like nothing matters. It's a form of depression.

It happens when we go and go and go and never stop to fill up our own tank.

There have been times in my life that I just have absolutely no interest in doing what I get to do for work. I don't want to even think about it. You dread returning to work on Sundays.

I'd be enjoying the weekend. We'd be having a blast. Until, all of a sudden, it would hit me like a ton of bricks. BAM! It stopped me dead in my tracks, right at about noon on Sunday. I'd feel the sense of impending doom.

There's a name for this phenomenon. In modern times, it's known as the 'Sunday Scaries.' It's a relatively new phenomenon. You have to wonder why.

Throughout history, this little piece of weekend anxiety never reared its ugly head. There could be many reasons for that. But mostly, I believe it's because life used to move at a much slower pace. Breaks were built in. Even now, when we're resting, we're working. With email and smartphones, many of us tend to take our work everywhere. And with more and more people working remotely from home, we just can't seem to escape it.

I'm just as guilty. What happens when we do this? Not only do we miss what's happening in the world around us with some of the people that matter most, but we drain our batteries even further when they should be recharging.

Here's a promise. It's a fact; when you put your phone down, the world will be there when you come back. And you may even find that you didn't miss all that much.

**Good Plan**

**Digital Detox** - Schedule your digital detox today. Put it on your calendar. Pick a day or the weekend to put your phone away. I promise it will all be here when you come back to it. And you will feel even better than before.

## 9

## LISTEN TO THE EXPERTS

### Do Not Worry

*"Therefore I tell you, do not worry
    about your life, what you will eat
    or drink; or about your body, what
    you will wear. Is not life more
    than food, and the body more than
    clothes? Look at the birds of the
    air; they do not sow or reap or
    store away in barns, and yet your
    heavenly Father feeds them. Are
    you not much more valuable than
    they? Can any one of you by
    worrying add a single hour to
    your life?*
*"And why do you worry about
    clothes? See how the flowers of*

*the field grow. They do not labor or spin. Yet I tell you that not even Solomon in all his splendor was dressed like one of these. If that is how God clothes the grass of the field, which is here today and tomorrow is thrown into the fire, will he not much more clothe you—you of little faith? So do not worry, saying, 'What shall we eat?' or 'What shall we drink?' or 'What shall we wear?' For the pagans run after all these things, and your heavenly Father knows that you need them. But seek first his kingdom and his righteousness, and all these things will be given to you as well. Therefore do not worry about tomorrow, for tomorrow will worry about itself. Each day has enough trouble of its own.*

— -MATTHEW 6:25

The mantra during all of 2020 was "listen to the experts." But what happens when the experts get it wrong? It happens more often than they'd have you believe. There's a whole industry devoted to these so-called experts. TV news networks prop up talking heads in an attempt to sway public opinion. But does anybody care about getting it right?

Let's take a look at their record. The "experts" once thought the Earth was flat. Some still do. In fact, it was heresy to suggest anything else. The same so-called expert class never thought man would fly.

Others thought man would never break the 4-minute mile. History is littered with the many times the trusted authorities were wrong.

In a day and age when we have every single bit of information at our fingertips, we can access it all in the blink of an eye, at lightning speed. There is no shortage of data. We live in an Information Age where we are being fed a steady diet of info. Constant notifications are pinging on our phones, and we're gorging on data. But the one thing that seems to be in short supply these days is the key to unlocking it all. *Wisdom*.

They say knowledge is power but what is knowledge without the ability to decipher it all?

> *"Above all else, guard your heart, for it is the wellspring of life."*

> — PROVERBS 4:23

We heard a lot about trusting the experts, the

science, and data all through 2020. But no one talks about the tool that we should use to cut through all of the chatter. Discernment.

These days, there's more knowledge available to us than ever before. There's more computing power in the palm of your hand than the giant computers used to send man to the moon in the 60s. Smartphones are millions of times faster than the guidance computers used on the Apollo missions. You might even be floored to hear that even our USB-C chargers have more juice than the same computer used to send man from Earth 365,000 km to the moon and back safely.

But all of the knowledge in the world, or even on the moon, is useless without wisdom.

Facts, data, and numbers can all be manipulated, and they often are. In a day and age when it seems like up is down and left is right, we're constantly told words don't mean what they used to. Everything is being redefined. Chaos rules the day.

Without a solid base built on rock, none of us stand a chance. That's why we need to get our house in order and build it on a foundation of faith. Truth. The Word.

Every morning I spend a little time with God. I start my day with Him. As I mentioned earlier, I take the time to focus on what matters first. I write in my journal, pray and read. Whether it's a good devotional book, I love <u>Jesus Calling</u>, or a good piece from the Bible, I like to soak it in because it's the Truth.

I started a practice a few years back that may be helpful to you too. I read a chapter from the book of Proverbs every day. There are 31 chapters, and they read quickly. It only takes just a few minutes each day, and you're soaking in the wisdom of the ages.

This time spent with the Word, in prayer, and journaling has helped give me the foundation to know what's real and what's baloney.

If you're reading this book, chances are you have a well-defined BS meter. In talk radio, it's nearly impossible to fool the audience. In most cases, the folks listening to the radio are just as informed as the host and, in some cases, know even more! They are well-read and have a good grasp of many subjects. But in recent years, much misinformation and disinformation has crept in. Conspiracy theories abound. Some have even proven to be true! With this type of landscape, it's more important than ever to be rooted in the truth.

Often people will ask me about certain situations. I heard this frequently around the election in 2020. "What's going to happen?" People would often wonder. My response is always the same. Honest but based in truth. "I don't know. All I know is God is still in control, and He's still on the throne." That response comes from the foundation of faith I plant and cultivate each day. And a certain peace just flows from it.

During the 77days we spent in the hospital with momma and baby, I felt the same way. It's impossible to have all of the answers. But you don't need to know it all when you see what matters most.

The experts can be wrong, or they may be right. Even a broken clock is right twice a day. But the honest truth comes from a much different place. Tune out the so-called know-it-all experts and dial in the wisdom that comes from a much higher place.

## Good plan

1. Read God's Word
2. Ask Him for guidance
3. Listen for the answer
4. Do what He says!

## 10

## ONE BITE AT A TIME

I was out of breath, in pain. I could barely walk to the mailbox and back without suffering the consequences of my poor diet and lifestyle choices. At one point, I tipped the scales at nearly 400 pounds.

As someone who has dropped the weight, I understand that *weight* can be physical, mental, emotional, and spiritual.

And believe it or not, they're all connected.

I won't go into great detail here about dropping the weight, but you can do it. And when you take the first step, the dominoes will eventually begin to fall. It's inevitable.

I started my journey to drop the physical pounds like most journeys, with the first step.

In the beginning, I was in pain. Before I knew it, I was consistently walking every day and often hitting 10,000 steps. Eventually, I moved on to Boot-camp-style workouts.

Today, the idea of moving is a significant part of my daily routine. I make it a must every day. It's non-negotiable. Too cold? Doesn't matter. Don't feel like it? Doesn't matter. It's raining? Doesn't matter. I either walk or work out for at least 30 minutes every day. Like Newton said, "A body in motion tends to stay in motion." And the opposite is true too. That's why I never allow myself to stay still for too long.

Moving has undoubtedly helped me drop the physical pounds, without a doubt. But along with the number on the scale, I *feel* like a new man too.

You won't believe what it can do for your physical and mental health.

By moving daily, you set yourself up to seize the opportunities that come your way every day. To seize those opportunities, you must first be able to *see* them.

They are all around you—part of the Good News. God is always at work. All around us. In every moment. The many miracles working inside your very body at any given moment are proof of this concept. Your heart beats, and you constantly breathe without even having to think about it.

But you are now.

Because I mentioned it.

That's more proof of the RAS at work, like I mentioned before.

The power of awareness is one thing. It's important to know what you're up against. But it's even more critical that you take action and move!

Just like the thought of losing over 100 pounds, many challenges we face daily can seem daunting. But they don't have to be. Something magical happens in the blink of an eye. It really is miraculous. When a decision is made, it's almost like flipping a switch.

*Q: How do you eat an elephant?*

*A: One bite at a time*

The old joke is funny but true. Just like in any endeavor, no matter how monumental, you must start small to accomplish mighty tasks. Where do you start? *Where you are.*

It's not enough to know the good news. It's not enough to understand the world. But we must use that knowledge, apply wisdom, and take action. Together, we can make a difference in our own lives and, more importantly, in the lives of others.

Each of us is called to a particular purpose. We have a great destiny to fulfill. Every individual has unique God-given talents, gifts, and abilities that directly align with their own calling—your reason for living.

If this sounds like biting off more than you can chew, don't worry because you don't have to take this all on at once.

I couldn't even fathom when I was close to 400

pounds doing some of the activities that I do now daily. But here I am. And today, I couldn't imagine *not* doing them. The point here is no matter what giant you face; God is bigger.

No matter what you plan to achieve, you can do it. You don't need to know-how. You just need to have the God-given desire and inspiration. Couple that with faith, and mighty mountains can be moved. You must only be willing to take the first step.

## Good plan

What have you been putting off for far too long? What can you do right now to take the first bite of that elephant? Take that first step, and the rest of the pieces will fall together.

## 11

## THE CALL

*"I've waited for this day for 40 years."*

A few years back, when the state of Indiana opened adoption records, it was the perfect timing to rekindle the search and dig in. As far back as I can remember, I've always known I was adopted. My parents told me at a very early age. I always planned on finding her, but I never knew exactly how it would all work out. I just knew that it would.

I can still remember the day it came in the mail. I opened the mailbox and saw the state seal. I knew exactly what it was. I ripped the letter open, and there it was. It was staring me in the face. My mother's name. My weight. All of the things that up until this point had been a mystery.

Minutes later, I was on the phone with a friend

of mine who does private detective work. He found her within an hour.

*"Are you sitting down?"*

He began to tell her everything. She interrupted and said, *"maybe I should've told you that I was driving!?"*

We talked for hours the next day. They flew by as she revealed all of the details of her life and the stories of family that I never knew. I had a brother! An entire family that I never knew existed until now.

There is an inevitable part of any process that can pose a bit of a challenge. It's almost the test of whether we want it bad enough or not. It's called the "messy middle." It's the spot where things can get frustrating. You've made your decision; you've taken action. And now, somewhere in the middle, you find yourself seemingly stuck.

The truth is, you're not stuck. You're transitioning. You're in between the old and the new. Chances are you are moving from one paradigm to another. World-renowned author and speaker Bob Proctor has talked about this concept through the years in his countless books and trainings.

He calls the messy middle the *"Terror Barrier."*

A paradigm is essentially any set of ideas and beliefs that we continue to believe daily.

It's our programming. The way we're wired.

Your subconscious mind is responsible for many many things that happen on autopilot every single minute of every day. Your breathing occurs without a single conscious thought. Your heart beats without you having to tell it to consciously! What a miraculous and glorious thing our body is.

As great as this is, sometimes these thoughts, concepts, & ideas don't always serve us. Just when we're about to move from one place to another, our subconscious mind kicks in and says.. *"Wait a minute! If you do this, you're going to get hurt! Or worse!"*

Just like when you were taught as a child that you don't talk to strangers, you look both ways when crossing the street, or not to touch a hot stove, your programming kicks in and says if you cross this line, pain is on the way. It's a survival mechanism.

So, how do you change your programming?

It's simple.

Proctor says two things can change a paradigm, An emotional and dramatic event, like 9/11 or constant spaced repetition. In other words, the continuous repeating of the idea over and over again.

This simple concept can shine some light on how news and media work to form ideas and get a nation to accept them without rationally thinking about them.

*"A lie told often enough becomes the truth"*

— -VLADIMIR LENIN

Yes, governments, media, and even individuals are guilty of this. The subconscious mind has no idea of what is true and false. It doesn't care. And while that can be a very dangerous thing, it can also be of great benefit to you too.

The lies that you tell yourself repeatedly can be just as dangerous as what mass media may be programming you with daily.

The difference here is that you can reprogram yourself at any moment. You can choose.

If you want to lose weight, you can reprogram yourself to believe that you're an athlete instead of the lie that you're just "big-boned." There is no such thing.

Have you ever heard the phrase, when it rains, it pours?

It's offend repeated by folks who believe that bad things happen all of the time, and when they do, they happen over and over again. These people have found themselves in a self-fulfilling prophecy—a real rut.

But just like these individuals, others in the world just seem to have the "Midas touch." Anything they touch turns to gold. Instead of a rut, they're living in the groove! It's a constant state of flow. Everything comes with such ease.

These two individuals are using the very same principles and concepts. Only they're using them in their opposite.

It's all in their programming.

The night before, I talked to my mother for the first time I had gone to bed. We were going to talk the next day. She would call me. She wanted to tell my brother before we spoke. They are very close, and she wanted to share the news.

I woke up in the middle of the night and did what I probably shouldn't have done. But I was tempted to roll over and grab my phone. I just wondered. What if I typed her name into the search bar on social media. And so I did. There she was. I saw her face for the first time. We could be twins. I scrolled through the pictures of other relatives. I saw cousins and uncles and aunts and grandparents.

For the first time in my life, I was staring at people who looked like me.

That's when it hit me. A thought passed over me. These pictures were of people that weren't really overweight. I had struggled with it all of my life. Part of me had just accepted that maybe I was supposed to. But in this moment, something must've clicked because I thought to myself, *perhaps I don't have to be.* And then the big realization, *maybe I'm not supposed to be!?*

That is a paradigm shift in a heartbeat. That very moment led to a series of events that culminated with me dropping neary 100 pounds. The weight was finally lifted. Physically and beyond. My old programming was rewired. The switch was flipped.

What determines the choices we make and who we become?

Is it genetic? Is it just luck?

There's a great story about two twins who found themselves at very different places later on in life. They had each taken polar opposite paths. One man found himself in jail and the other a very successful, wealthy, and respected member of his community.

When a reporter sat down with each man to discover why they were so different, he found something astonishing.

The first of the two brothers, who was locked up in the clink, told the reporter. "I came from a broken marriage; I experienced abuse, my father was a drunk. *I had to fail because I had no choice.*"

Upon hearing his reasoning, one could certainly come to see that indeed he had a point.

But when the reporter sat down with the other brother, what he heard blew him away.

How did he get here? The wealthy and successful twin explained, "I came from a broken marriage, I experienced abuse, my father was a drunk. *I had to succeed because I had no choice.*"

The truth is that both men were wrong. They each had a choice. They both had the exact same circumstances and even the same DNA, but both made different choices.

No matter what we're going through in life, we each have the power to respond to our circumstances. We have the freedom to make our own choices.

Victor Frankl's 1946 book, *"Man's Search For Meaning,"* directly deals with this concept. Frankl was a psychologist who survived the horrors of Nazi Germany. He saw many perish in concentration camps during WWII. What he found was powerful —identifying a purpose in life and imagining its outcome directly affected each prisoner.

His theory says that the meaning of life is found in every moment of living; life never ceases to have meaning, even in suffering and death.

It's absolutely astounding how something so profound can come out of such a horrific experience. It proves the theory itself.

Even though the prisoners were locked up, tortured, and eventually killed, they still had the freedom to choose how they chose to see the world and even the horror they experienced. No one, not even the sadistic guards, could take that away.

That's a powerful truth. We have the power to choose. That's the ultimate freedom. And because freedom comes from God, only we can give our freedom away.

I don't know why certain roads led me to where I find myself today. But I choose to see God's hand in it all.

I can't imagine the pain that my mother experienced all of those years. The last time she saw me, I was two days old. A nurse had come into her room to check on her, and she asked, *"do you think I could hold him?"* Her room had a window that overlooked the nursery. The nurse left to ask and never came back. Eventually, someone closed the curtain, and that was the last she saw of me.

It still chokes me up to think about how she had those last moments seared into her brain. I don't understand it all but what I do know is that the self-less sacrifice she made blessed me.

It broke generational bondage that can only be explained in one way.

I grew up with loving parents. They'd watched their friends and family having children all around them, but they suffered miscarriage after miscarriage. They couldn't have children of their own. Or at least that's what they believed until they brought me home.

Less than a year to the day my brother was born. A gift locked inside of a blessing.

There was one tiny request my mother made when she decided to give me a better life. She simply asked that the family who raised me would bring me to church. How could a young mother at 17 have the wisdom to ask? What were the odds the family would even honor it?

They did. My parents hadn't been to church in years. But as my brother and I got old enough, they started taking us. I grew up going to Sunday school and learning about God.

Those seeds, no matter how small, were planted all of those years ago.

No matter where you find yourself stuck at this very moment, you have the power to choose. Where you go and how you see the world. Is it all happening to you or for you?

This very notion can and will determine your outcome today and in every way. What if just as it appeared, things were falling apart, they were really falling together?

No one but God could see the beauty that would come out of the ashes at that moment.

He has the power to transform all things. No matter how bad or how lost we feel.

The rest of the story is yet to be written, and you get to spread your own good news.

# CONCLUSION

*"She's gotta pass the car seat test."*

W hats' the car seat test? Maybe one of the easiest tests they will run on your baby in the NICU. It's also the one you look forward to the most because it's the last one your baby has to face.

What exactly is it? Your baby has to sit in her car seat for 90 minutes while strapped up to wires and monitors.

Our nurse told us to get something to eat. "You don't wanna be here for this. It really is boring." After 77 days in the hospital, even the most seemingly simple test carries the weight of the world. You can feel the pressure because if she passes, we get to take her home. If not, she has to wait it out a few days and take it again.

Off to the cafeteria, we went to grab some lunch. When we walked back in, there she was—sleeping like the proverbial baby. She passed with flying colors.

I'll never forget the day we got to bring her home. It was the day after Lizzie's birthday. Our story is filled with miraculous synchronicities.

But that's par for the course. God is always speaking; the real question is, are we listening?

Over the last several pages, I've tried to lay out the good news. I wanted to share my secrets to finding the calm to hear His voice as He speaks to me.

Yes, the world is in a constant state of chaos. Evil abounds. But the good news is, God is still on the throne.

It's easy to lose sight of this. That's why I've laid out some simple steps to get you focused on what matters most.

1. **Thank God** - Start your day with a grateful heart, and you will find God present throughout every moment. You can train yourself to see the good in the world when you focus on the blessings you already experience.
2. **Unplug from the noise -** Schedule your digital detox. Put it on the calendar now. Evaluate how the media you

consume each day makes you feel. If you
need to cut it back, try it for a week or so
and see how you feel. I guarantee you
won't believe how good you can feel after
a fast.

3. **Know that good wins -** It doesn't
   matter what chapter we're on. We know
   how this story ends. Stay in the Word.
   Read the Bible and pray. Ask God to
   show you the good in the world as you
   thank Him for each blessing.

When you put these simple steps into practice,
you'll begin to experience a peace that surpasses any
circumstance you might be facing.

> *"I can do all things through Christ who strengthens
> me."*
>
> — -PHILIPPIANS 4:13 NKJV

I pray that these steps equip you for the battles
that we face each day and help you find joy in every
moment when you focus on the truth that God loves
you, is for you, and will never leave you.

Get Good News sent to your email at
JustinBarclay.com/goodnews

# ABOUT THE AUTHOR

*Photo: Justin with wife Lizzie and their
daughter, Ada Grace.*

Justin's parents will tell you he  was born with a
microphone in his hand. So, it's no wonder his radio
career started even before he was out of high school.

Justin's been heard in major markets all across the country including Philadelphia, Detroit, Tampa, Cincinnati, & Louisville; but fondly calls West Michigan (Grand Rapids) home.

He's a frequent guest host for the nationally syndicated Glenn Beck program heard on over 300 radio stations coast to coast.

He can be heard today engaging guests and listeners in lively conversations about national and local topics all while talking about what matters most in West Michigan.

Justin has won multiple 'Awards for Broadcast Excellence' from The Michigan Association of Broadcasters and is honored to continue serving the community on and off of the legendary airwaves of WOOD Radio.